Jokes Not To Tell Your Gran

Jokes NOT TO TELL YOUR GRAN

Gill Brown

Illustrated by David Mostyn

RED FOX

A Red Fox Book

Published by Random Century Children's Books
20 Vauxhall Bridge Road, London SW1V 2SA
A division of the Random Century Group

London Melbourne Sydney Auckland
Johannesburg and agencies throughout the world

Red Fox edition 1991

Text © Gill Brown 1991
Illustrations © Oxford Graphics 1991

The right of Gill Brown and David Mostyn to be identified as the
author and illustrator of this work respectively has been asserted by
them in accordance with the Copyright, Designs and Patents Act, 1988.

This book is sold subject to the condition that it shall not, by way of trade
or otherwise, be lent, resold, hired out, or otherwise circulated without
the publisher's prior consent in any form of binding or cover other than
that in which it is published and without a similar condition including this
condition being imposed on the subsequent purchaser.

Set in Century Oldstyle
Typeset by Getset (BTS) Ltd
Printed and bound in Great Britain by
Cox & Wyman Ltd, Reading, Berks.

ISBN 0 09 974960 2

Contents
Don't ask!

ALSO BY DAVID MOSTYN AND PUBLISHED BY RED FOX, "HOW TO DRAW CRAZY CARTOONS."

Dedicated to Grannys wherever they are.

—Cleaning their false teeth in public and sitting on the cat

MY GRAN →

Granny was shopping for a new dress and couldn't find anything she liked. Finally she asked, 'Do you think I could try on that dress in the window?'
'I think it would be much better if you tried it on in the changing-room,' replied the assistant.

ESKIMO CHILD: Where does your Gran come from?
SECOND ESKIMO CHILD: Alaska.
FIRST ESKIMO CHILD: Don't worry, I'll ask her myself.

Why did it take so long to wind up Grandad's estate?
Because he left thirty grandfather clocks.

Did you hear about the granny who plugged her electric blanket into the toaster by mistake, and spent the night popping out of bed?

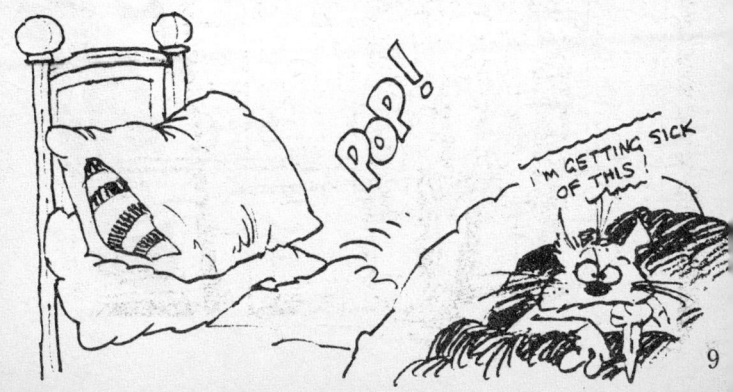

Grandad was eating in a restaurant when he bit hard on a chicken bone and broke his false teeth. 'Don't worry,' said the waiter. 'My brother can fit you with a new set right away.'

Grandad didn't believe him, but sure enough the man returned shortly with a set of teeth that fitted him perfectly. 'It's astonishing,' said Grandad. 'They fit me perfectly. Your brother must be an excellent dentist.'

'Oh, he's not a dentist,' replied the waiter. 'He's an undertaker.'

GRANNY: Eat up your spinach, Caroline, it's good for growing children.
CAROLINE: But who wants to grow children?

Grandad was getting a bit forgetful, and complained that the match wouldn't light as he tried to get his fire going.

'What's the matter with it?' asked his son.

'I don't know,' replied Grandad. 'It worked a moment ago.'

CHEEKY CHARLIE: Were you in Noah's Ark, Grandpa?
GRANDPA: Of course not.
CHEEKY CHARLIE: Then how did you escape drowning?

FIND GRANNY AND GRANDPA

Despite appearances, there is only one GRANNY and only one GRANDPA hidden in this word grid. The words may read across, up or down, or diagonally, either forwards or backwards, but they are both in straight lines.

A	P	D	N	A	G	R	A	N	N	P	A
P	N	A	R	G	R	A	N	N	D	P	P
D	A	D	G	R	A	N	D	A	P	A	D
N	G	G	R	R	N	G	R	R	A	Y	N
A	R	R	A	A	A	A	N	A	N	N	G
Y	A	A	N	N	N	N	Y	N	D	R	R
D	N	N	D	G	N	N	N	N	A	G	A
R	D	N	A	G	A	N	N	Y	R	N	N
A	A	A	P	D	R	Y	G	R	N	A	D
N	G	A	P	D	N	A	R	G	D	N	N
N	R	D	P	A	G	R	A	R	A	N	Y
Y	N	N	A	D	A	D	N	D	G	N	N

CYCLE RIDE

How many differences can you spot between these two pictures?

DOCTOR: Did you drink your medicine after your bath?
GRAN: I didn't have much room for the medicine after drinking the bath!

GRAN: Nature is wonderful, you know.
FREDDIE: Why do you say that?
GRAN: Well, she couldn't have known that people were going to invent spectacles, but look where she put our ears.

Gran fell down on the ice and broke her leg, and was in a plaster cast for several months. When the time came to remove it, she asked the doctor excitedly, 'Does this mean I can go up the stairs again?'

'Yes,' he replied.

'What a relief,' replied Gran. 'It was getting to be hard work climbing up the drainpipe.'

> *Where do you find a little, old, grey Grandpa?*
> It depends where you leave him.

GRAN: Come here, Belinda, and watch the cuckoo come out of the cuckoo clock when it strikes the hour.
BELINDA: Can we then go and watch Grandfather come out of the grandfather clock?

Why didn't Jimmy want to play cowboys and Indians with his Grandpa?
Because his Grandpa had already been scalped.

Did you hear about the granny who still reckoned everything in pounds, shillings and pence? She didn't see the point of decimal coinage.

GRAN: Doctor, I think I'm shrinking!
DOCTOR: You'll just have to be a little patient.

HOW MANY GRANNIES?

If a granny:
1. Wears a hat
2. Has grey hair in a bun
3. Wears specs
4. Wears a plain black cardigan over a plain white blouse
5. Wears a dark patterned skirt that covers her knees
6. Wears dark stockings and flat shoes

how many grannies are there in the picture?

WHY ARE YOU WATCHING ME?
I'M WAITING FOR YOU TO DO YOUR FROG IMPRESSION

WHAT DO YOU MEAN? I'VE NEVER DONE A FROG IMPRESSION IN MY LIFE.
THAT'S A PITY, DAD SAID WE'D GET £20,000 IF YOU CROAKED.

GRAN, DOING CROSSWORD: I've been trying to think of this word for two weeks.
CLEVER CLARA: How about a fortnight?

STINKER: Mum, there's a lady at the door collecting for the Old People's Home. Shall I give her Grandpa?

FREDDIE: Grandpa, do you believe in free speech?
GRANDPA: Certainly, my boy.
FREDDIE: May I use your telephone then?

MANDY: I've borrowed Grandad's bugle.
ANDY: But you can't play it.
MANDY: Neither can he while I've got it.

DOCTOR: It's best to take a hot bath just before retiring.
GRANDPA: OK, Doc, I'll take one in six months' time.

PATCHWORK PUZZLE

How many extraordinary things is Gran sewing into her patchwork?

A fitness freak was boasting about the enormous weights he could lift.

'That's nothing,' said Henry. 'My Gran can lift over a thousand pounds.'

'I don't believe it,' said the fitness freak.

'It's true,' replied Henry. 'She's a cashier at the bank in the High Street.'

Knock, knock.
Who's there?
Dishwasher.
Dishwasher who?
Dishwasher the way I spoke before I had false teeth.

Why is it easy to break into Grandad's house?
Because his gait is broken and his locks are few.

JANE: My Grandad died from drinking varnish by mistake.
WAYNE: How awful!
JANE: Yes, but he had a lovely finish.

GRAN, ON HER FIRST FLIGHT: Er, how often do these planes crash?
STEWARDESS: Only once, Madam.

GRAN: What are you going to do when you grow up, Jim?
JIM: Drive a double-decker bus.
GRAN: Well, none of us will stand in your way.

GRAN: Have another piece of my sponge cake, dear.
HONEST HETTIE: No thanks, Gran, it tasted a bit old.
GRAN: That's funny. I bought a new sponge from the chemist this morning.

When Stinker's Gran took him to a big department store she lost him, and then found him gazing down at the escalator.

'Are you all right?' she asked.

'Sure,' replied Stinker. 'I'm just waiting for my chewing-gum to come round again.'

WHAT?

1. Does a granny use to make fish and chips?
2. Game does a grandpa play on a cricket pitch?
3. Is Princess Diana's granny-in-law's first name?
4. Do grannies do in the rain?
5. Does a granny's tape measure measure?
6. Animal would a grandpa like to be on a cold day?
7. Sort of granny wears glasses?
8. Would you do with granny's chocolate cake?
9. Does grandpa grow in his garden?
10. Does grandpa do when his nose runs?

FAMILY PARTY

At a family gathering there were: one grandmother, one grandfather, five daughters, five sons, three mothers, three fathers, one granddaughter, one grandson, one son-in-law and one daughter-in-law. What is the minimum number of people who could have been present?

Granny Dean went to the post office to buy a stamp, and because she was having trouble fumbling with her money and her gloves, the man behind the counter stuck it on the letter for her.

'Hang on,' he said, 'you've written the address upside down.'

'I know,' said Granny Dean. 'It's going to my sister in Australia.'

Why was Grandad pleased to retire from his job in the bakery?
Because the work was so crummy.

Why couldn't the retired bank manager ride a bike?
He'd lost his balance.

> YOUR HAIR IS GETTING VERY GREY, SIR.
>
> I'VE BEEN WAITING SO LONG I'M NOT SURPRISED.

KATE: Where were you born, Gran?
GRAN: In the hospital, Kate.
KATE: Oh dear. What was the matter with you?

← A SNAKE WITH A BROKEN LEG

BIRD TABLE

The birds that visit Granny and Grandpa's bird table are drawn here from the letters that make up their names. Can you work out which kinds of birds they are?

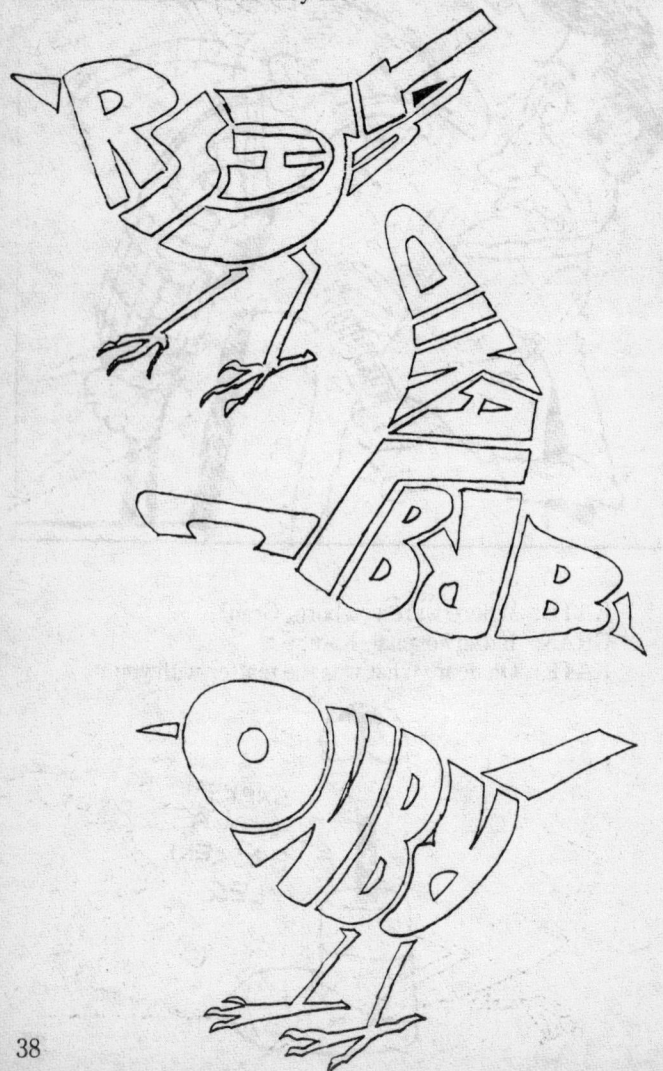

38

"US BUDGIES NEVER GET PROPER MEDIA COVERAGE"

GRANDAD PERKINS: My rheumatism is so much better since you told me to avoid damp conditions, Doctor.
DOCTOR: That's good news, Mr Perkins. It was about a year ago, wasn't it?
GRANDAD PERKINS: Yes, and I feel so much better I wondered if it would be all right for me to have a bath now?

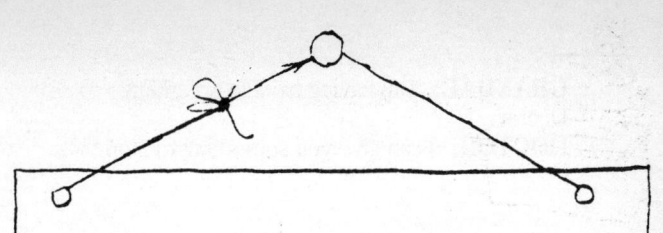

How do you keep a very old granny from dying?
Make her stay in the living-room.

What does a bald Grandad have?
A very wide parting.

Gran had done a painting of her husband. 'Why did you paint him in oils?' asked her neighbour.
    'Because he looks like a sardine,' replied Gran.

Why did Stinker's eccentric Grandad hide under the bed?
Because he thought he was a little potty.

GRANDAD: I'm having trouble breathing, Doctor.
DOCTOR: I can give you something to stop that.

When are racing cars like Grandads?
When they have vroomatism.

STINKER: My Gran's so old she's got one foot in the grate.
FREDDIE: Don't you mean the grave?
STINKER: No, the grate. She says she wants to be cremated.

Freddie took his Granny to the cinema. He asked her if she could see all right. Yes, she replied. He asked if anyone was blocking her view. No, she replied. And he asked her if her seat was quite comfortable. Oh yes, she replied, 'Mind changing places?' he asked.

Darren was telling Sharon about his grandfather. He had once worked as a carpenter, but had then gone blind. But, amazingly, a few weeks ago, he had regained his sight.

'Amazing,' said Sharon. 'How did he manage to do that?'

'It was easy,' said Darren. 'He just picked up his chisel and saw.'

TONGUE-TWISTER

Try saying this quickly:

> GRAN'S GREY GEESE GRAZE GREEDILY ON GREEN GRASS AND GAZE GLEEFULLY AT GRAN'S GLANCE.

Knock, knock.
Who's there?
Granny.
Knock, knock.
Who's there?
Granny.
Knock, knock.
Who's there?
Aunty.
Aunty who?
Aunty glad I got rid of those grannies?

CRAZY, MIXED-UP GRANNIES!

Can you turn the letters of GRANNIES into another word meaning 'pay'?

KATE: My Gran's a maniokleptic.
GLORIA: Don't you mean a kleptomaniac?
KATE: No, she doesn't steal, she walks backwards into shops and leaves things.

What should Granny and Grandad eat with their jacket potatoes?
Button mushrooms.

PICTURE STORY

These pictures tell a story — or they would do if you put them in the correct order. Can you sort them out?

46

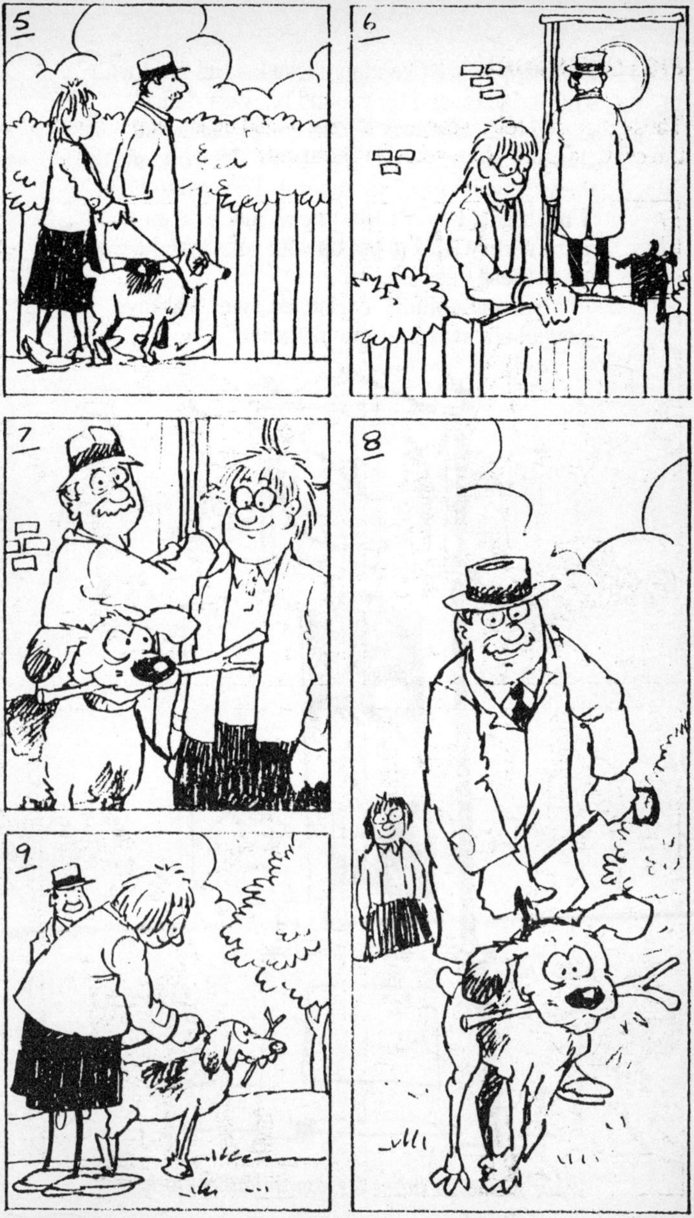
5
6
7
8
9

For many years Grandma Wrinkles had lived with Ted and Joan, and they found her very difficult to get on with. She was always complaining, and always bad-tempered. Eventually she died, and on the way home from her funeral, Ted said to Joan, 'I'm afraid if I didn't love you so much I'd have found it very hard to put up with your grandmother for all these years.'

'*My* grandmother!' exclaimed Joan. 'I always thought she was *your* grandmother!'

What's another name for a grandfather clock?
An old timer.

Grandma and Grandpa Herbert were persuaded by their family to take a trip to London on the train. They had never been on a train before, indeed, they had never left their home village.

As it was a long journey, and the start of a new and exciting time in their life, Grandma Herbert had bought them some bananas to eat on the train. They had never eaten bananas before, either.

Once they had got over the incredible speed at which the train travelled, they began to enjoy themselves, and decided to try one of the bananas. Grandpa unpeeled his first, and as he took a bite the train went into a tunnel.

'Mother!' he roared. 'Have you tried your banana yet?'

'No,' replied Grandma Herbert. 'I'm still unpeeling it.'

'Don't eat it,' cried Grandpa. 'I took one bite and went blind!'

KATE: Granny, why do you have three pairs of spectacles?
GRANNY: One pair is for reading, one pair is for watching television, and one pair is to help me find the other two.

Granny Jones, Granny Smith and Granny Taylor all met in town one blustery autumn afternoon.

'Windy, isn't it?' said Granny Jones.

'No, it's Thursday,' replied Granny Smith.

'So am I,' said Granny Taylor. 'Let's go and have a cup of tea.'

What's old and wrinkled and belongs to Grandma?
Grandpa.

GRANDAD POWER

Join the dots to see what this energetic Grandad is doing.

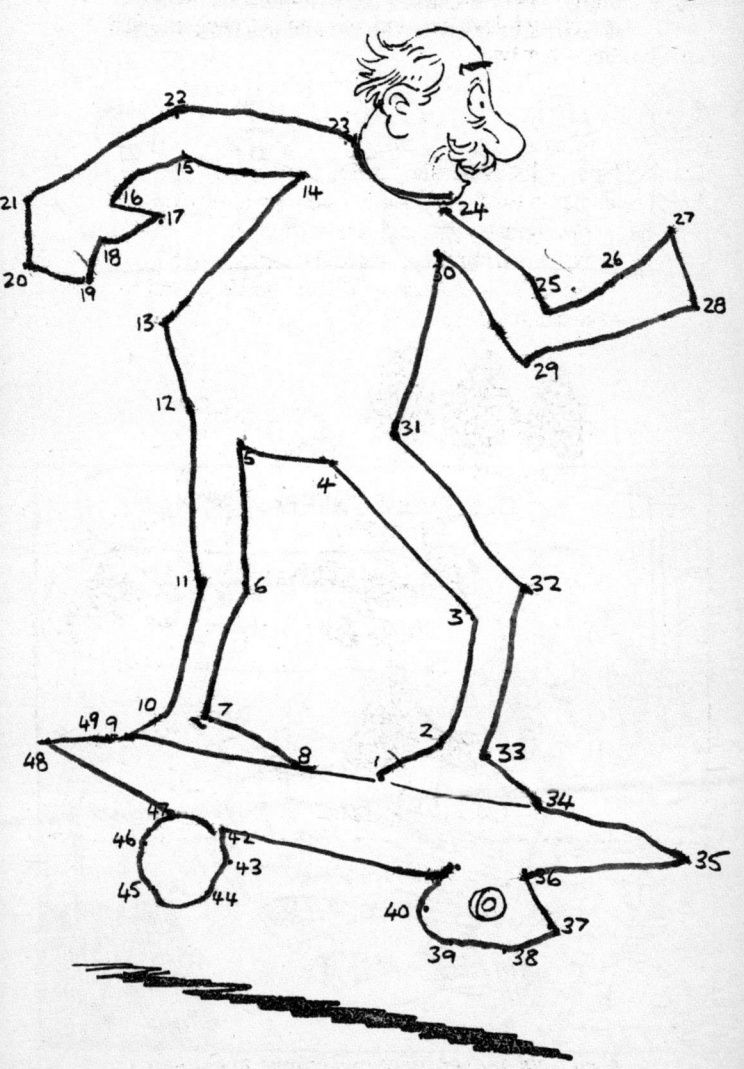

Granny and Grandpa Taylor were very, very old, and they lived in a very, very old tumbledown cottage. They reckoned the only reason it didn't fall down was because the woodworm held hands.

DOES YOUR WIFE MISS YOU?

NO. SHE'S A VERY GOOD SHOT. THAT'S WHY I'M HERE.

MRS BLENKINSOP: Now your husband's retired, what does he do? Has he a hobby?
GRANNY JONES: Yes, he's got a hobby he can stick to.
MRS BLENKINSOP: And what's that?
GRANNY JONES: He spends all day glued to the television.

What's the best way to avoid falling hair?
Jump out of the way!

THE GRANDMOTHER GAME

This is a good game to play on your own, or with family or friends, in which case they can either compete against each other or play as a team.

You will need as many sheets of squared paper and pencils as there are individual players, and you start by writing the word 'grandmother' in the middle of a sheet of paper. If the players are working together as a team they each take turns, otherwise each player has five minutes to think of as many words connected with 'grandmother' as possible and to interlock them with the original and subsequent words. The words might be connected with their own grandmother/s or with a typical grandmother.

If players are competing against each other, then the winner is the person who manages to interlock the greatest number of words.

In the example shown, the grandmother is called Elsie Ross. Her husband is called Bill, her daughter Wendy, she lives in Totnes and used to work as a nurse. She has white hair, blue eyes, a dog called Pinto, her hobby is sewing and her favourite television programme is *EastEnders*. Get the idea?

```
          D
          R
   G R A N D M O T H E R
          G
          O
          N A G
```

	B	L	U	E					D			
	I			A			P		O			
	L			S	E	W	I	N	G			
	L			T			N					
				E			T					
	G	R	A	N	D	M	O	T	H	E	R	
				D				O			O	
W	H	I	T	E				T			S	
E				R				N	U	R	S	E
N				S				E				L
D								S				S
Y												I
												E

GRANNY: Now, when my friends come round I want you to promise me that you won't drink your tea out of the saucer.
GRANDAD: What do you want me to drink it out of?
GRANNY: Out of the cup, of course.
GRANDAD: But if I do that the teaspoon will stick in my eye!

Grandad Murphy was a bit of a magician. Every time he went round the corner at the end of his street he turned into a pub.

Grandad Black met a man carrying a violin who asked him how to get to the Albert Hall.
'Practise,' replied Grandad Black.

GRAN: This lettuce doesn't taste very nice. Did you wash it, as I asked you to?
SUSANNAH: Oh, yes. If you look closely you can still see the soap on it.

Granny decided to buy herself a pair of high-heeled shoes for a special party. She explained to the young assistant what it was she wanted.

'Certainly, Madam. Walk this way,' said the young lady.

Gran glanced down at her shoes. 'If I buy any with heels that high, I might have to,' she replied.

WHO'S THIS?

HOW DID YOU COME TO FALL IN THE DUCKPOND?
I DIDN'T COME TO FALL IN THE DUCKPOND. I CAME TO FISH.

THIS IS MY GRANDPA!
HI GUYS!

DOCTOR: You seem to be in excellent health, Mrs Brown. Your pulse is as steady and regular as clockwork.
GRANNY BROWN: That's because you've got your hand on my watch.

GRANDAD: That roast beef we had yesterday was very tough. I hope you've given me something I can get my teeth into tonight.
GRANDMA: I certainly have. Here's a glass of water.

Why shouldn't old people choose their false teeth
by looking at them in shop windows?
Because it's not polite to pick your teeth in public.

'Your teeth are like the stars,' he said,
Pressing her hand so white.
He spoke the truth, for, like the stars
Her teeth came out at night.

Grandad Oliver was very careful with his money.
When he heard that the price of his favourite
newspaper was going up, he went out and bought
as many copies as he could that day.

BERTIE: Grandad, there's a man at the door with a moustache.
GRANDAD: Tell him I've already got one.

MAN TO SPIRITUALIST: I'd like to contact my grandfather who's been dead for ten years.
SPIRITUALIST: It'll cost you £30.
MAN: Can't you reverse the charges?

WOOL GATHERING

Which ball of wool is Granny knitting with at the moment?

TRACEY: My Gran had sent Grandad down the garden to pick some carrots for Sunday lunch when he had a heart attack and died.
STACEY: How terrible! What did she do?
TRACEY: What could she do? She got some peas out of the freezer.

BARBARA: My Grandad learnt to play the piano with his toes.
BRIAN: That's nothing! My Grandad's always fiddling with his beard.

HAIR ON A G-STRING

MIKE: How's your Grandad getting on in hospital?
SPIKE: Gran says he's taken a turn for the nurse.

GRANNY JONES: So you're not going to Rome for your holiday this year?
GRANNY SMITH: No, that was last year. This year we're not going to Spain.

MO: How did your Grandad lose his health?
FLO: Gran says it was drinking the health of others.

IT'S DISGUSTING!

Young Jimmy was having tea with his Gran.

'Would you like a biscuit?' she asked.

'Yes, please,' replied Jimmy.

'What good manners you have,' said his Gran. 'I do like to hear young people say "please" and "thank you".'

'I'll say them both if I can have a big slice of that cake,' replied Jimmy.

GRAN AND GRANDAD'S AGE

This simple calculator trick never fails to astonish people. Tell them before you start that you are going to perform a complicated sequence of calculations, which will result in Gran's age being shown on the left of the decimal point on the calculator, and Grandad's on the right of it. Then prove that you can do it!

All you do is:
1. Enter Gran's age on the calculator.
2. Multiply it by 2.
3. Add 5.
4. Multiply the total by 50.
5. Add Grandad's age.
6. Take away 250.
7. Divide the total by 100.

And, just as you predicted, Gran's age appears on the left of the decimal point, and Grandad's on the right!

SOFA, SO GOOD

Which of the pieces is the one missing from Granny's sofa?

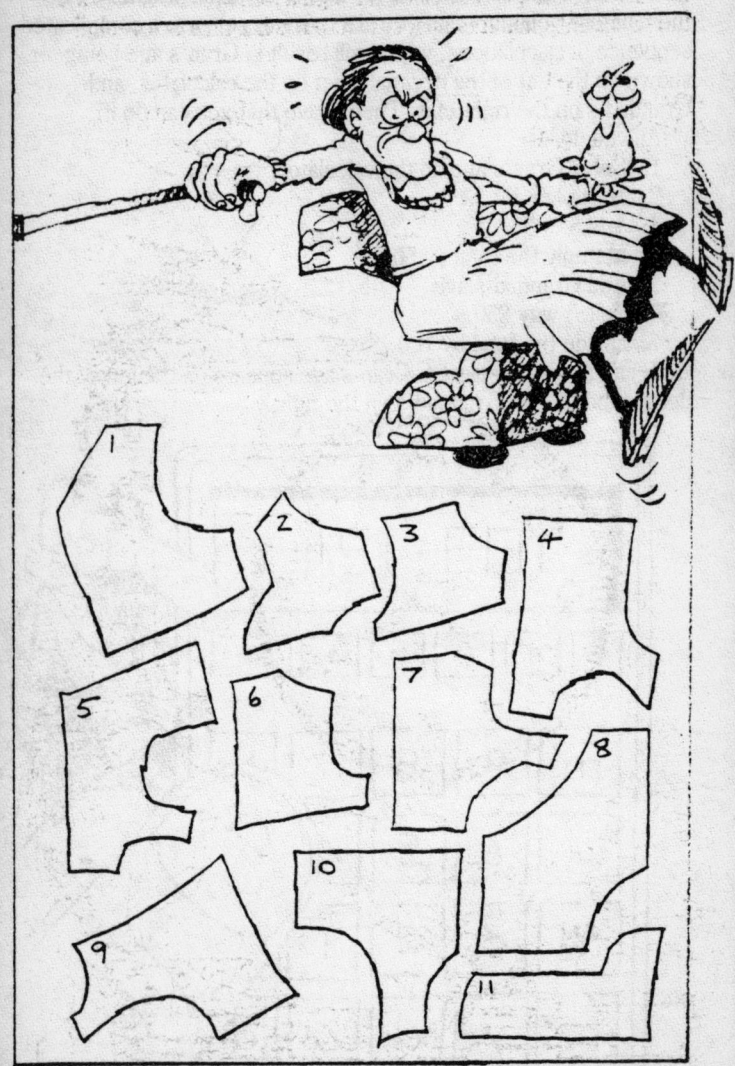

WHAT TIME IS IT?

Granny is looking at her clock through a mirror. It looks as if the time is twenty minutes past seven, but what time is it really?

"HOW'S YOUR NEW HEARING AID, GRANDPA? DOES IT WORK WELL?"

"NEVER EAT HERRINGS MY BOY. THE BONES STICK IN MY THROAT."

Grandad Perkins wasn't a very good driver, so he had his car painted blue on one side and white on the other. That way, he figured that if he had an accident the witnesses would spend all their time contradicting one another and he'd be let off.

"BLUE!"

"WHITE!"

STINKER: My Grandad has a glass eye.
KATE: How do you know?
STINKER: Oh, it came out once in conversation.

KATE: Grandad's hair is abdicating.
FREDDIE: What do you mean?
KATE: It's giving up the crown.

BARBER: How do you want your hair cut, sonny?
SONNY: Like Grandpa's – leave a hole on top.

There was an old granny of Leeds
Who ate a whole packet of seeds.
In a couple of hours
She had sprouted two flowers
And couldn't sit down for the weeds.

GRANNY KNOTS

Which of these pieces of string will pull into a knot?

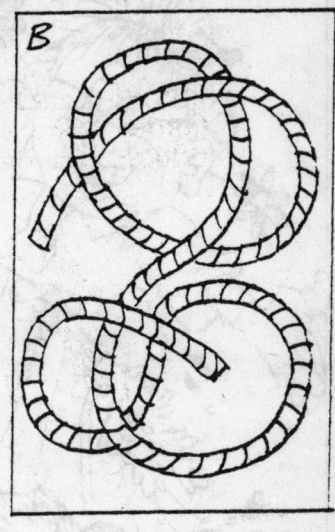

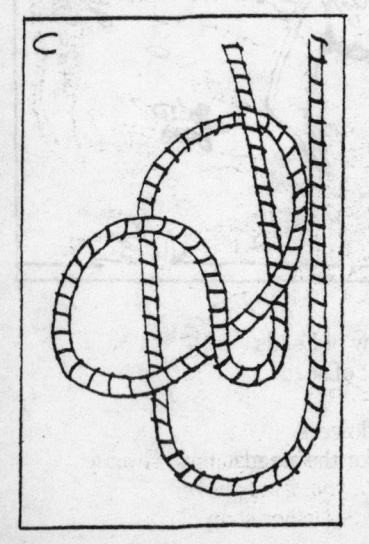

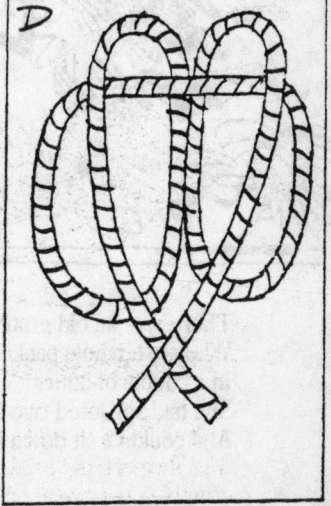

GRANNY: Don't eat your supper so quickly, Sandra.
SANDRA: But, Gran, I might lose my appetite if I slow down.

DARREN: How old is your Grandad?
SHARON: Approaching seventy.
DARREN: From which direction?

And while on the subject of table manners, Granny was always taught that a young lady never crumbles her bread or rolls in her soup.

OLD PUFFERS

At Kate's school sports day they had a grandad race. Three of the squares in this picture of it are identical – can you spot which they are? You can identify the squares by the letters across the top and the numbers down the side, so, for example, the top left-hand square is A1.

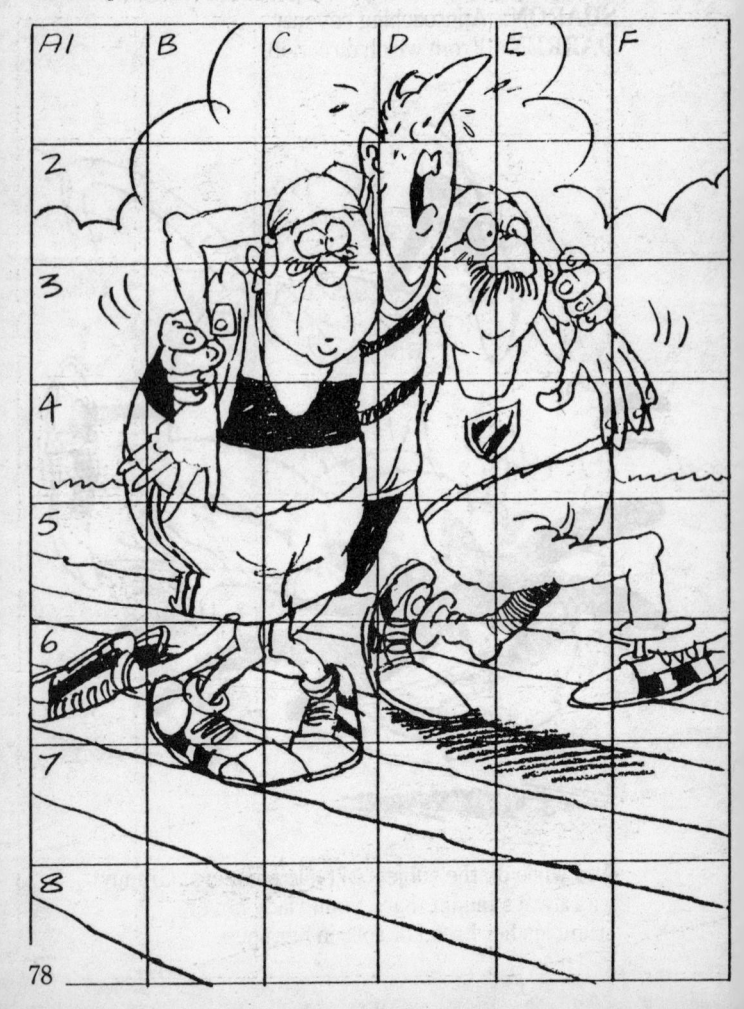

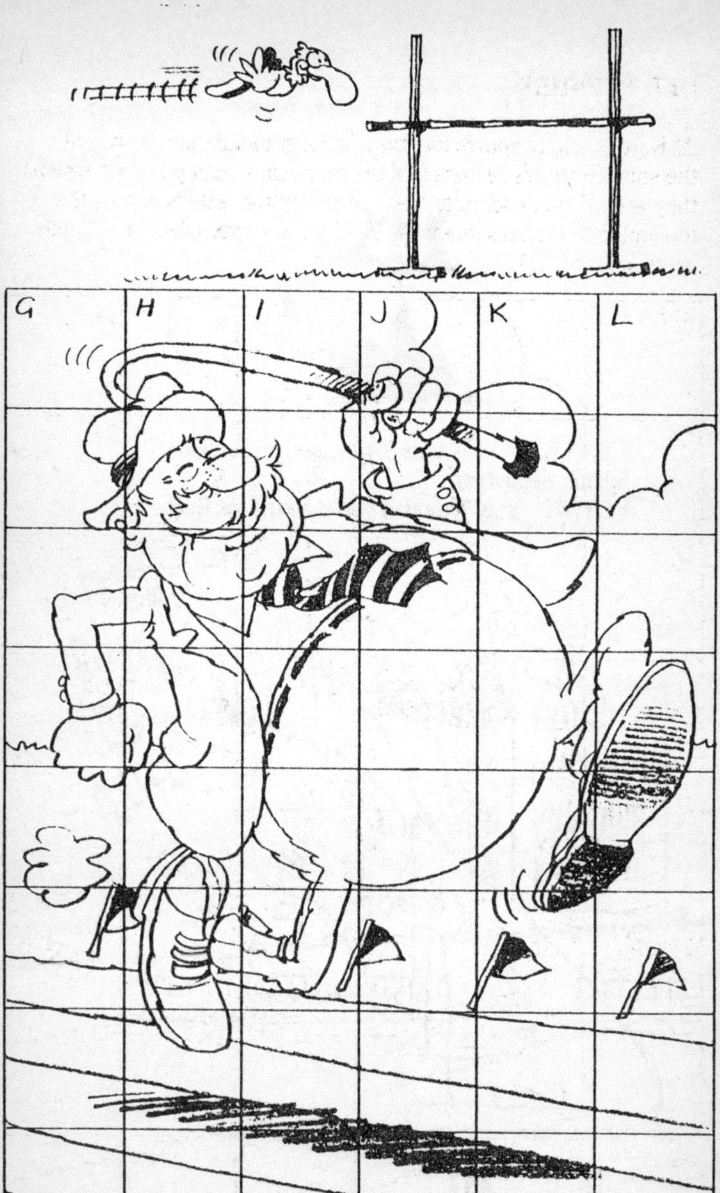
G
H
I
J
K
L

GRANDAD: Did you put the cat out, dear?
GRANDMA: No, was it on fire again?

LYNNE: Why is your Grandad's dog called Johann Sebastian?
FLYNN: You'd know if you'd heard his Bach.

81

SPOT THE SPECS

Gran is wearing one pair of specs, but how many more are hidden in the picture?

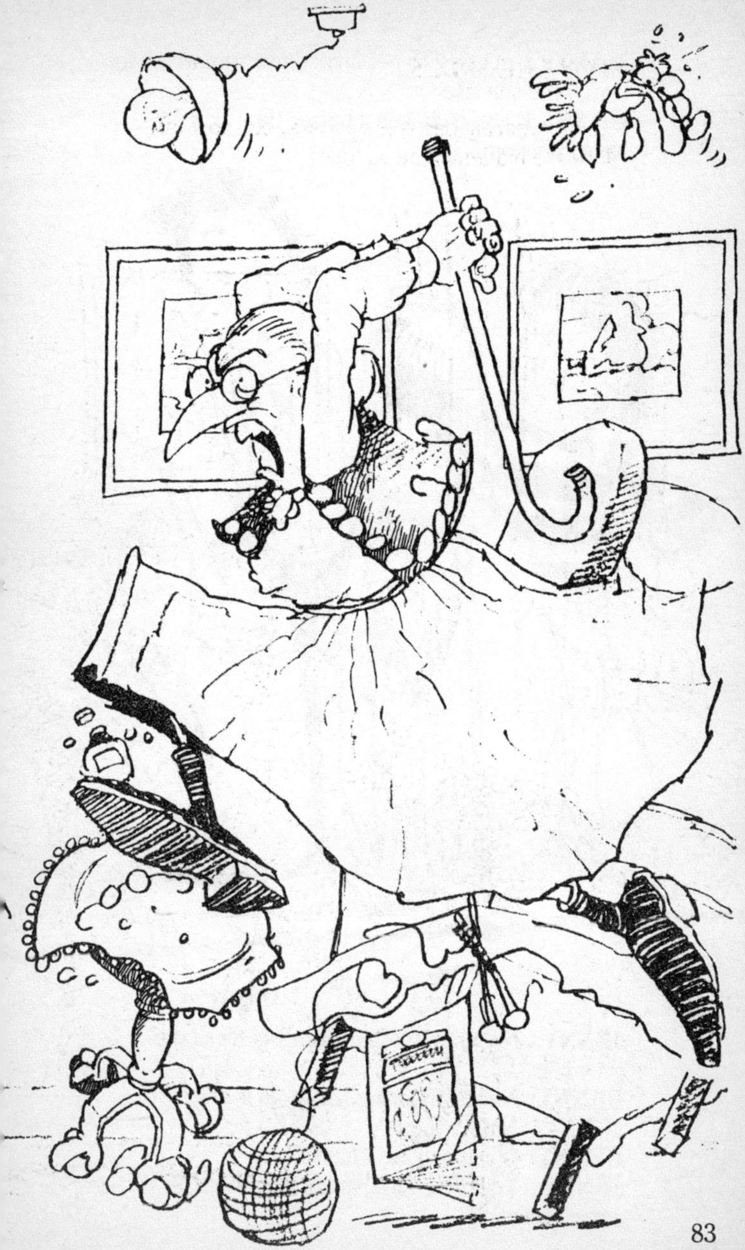

MARY: I'm going to get up at dawn tomorrow to watch the sun rise.
GRAN: If you'd chosen a better time I might have come with you.

JENNY: My grandmother hasn't got a single grey hair.
BENNY: That's amazing! How old is she?
JENNY: Ninety-four.
BENNY: What a wonderful old lady.
JENNY: Yes. The sad thing is that she's completely bald.

SLEEPING BEAUTY

Does your Granny or your Grandpa tend to fall asleep in front of the television? If so, here's a naughty trick you can play on him or her. All you have to do is to make a notice out of a piece of card, or even a large sheet of paper. Write on it 'Sleeping Beauty' or 'Man/Woman at Work – Do Not Disturb' or even '... Museum, Exhibit no. 123, Handle with Care' giving the name of your town. Everyone else will giggle as they go past poor Gran or Grandad, who, when they wake up, will wonder what the joke is. It might be as well for you not to be around at that time!

HARRY: Did Gran promise you something if you tidied your room?
LARRY: No, but she promised me something if I didn't!

DOCTOR: Now tell me, Granny Perkins, how you happened to burn both your ears.
GRANNY PERKINS: I was doing the ironing when the telephone rang, and I picked up the iron and put that to my ear by mistake.
DOCTOR: But you burnt both your ears!
GRANNY PERKINS: Yes, well as soon as I put the phone down it rang again!

> *How do you know when a Granny is getting old?*
> When her birthday cake costs less than the candles.

MOTHER: Susie, just pop round next door and see how old Granny Jenkins is, will you?
SUSIE (later): She's very cross, Mum. She says it's none of our business how old she is.

> MY GRANDFATHER'S SO OLD, WE GET DRIVEN BACK BY THE HEAT FROM HIS CANDLES.

> I'M SIX

WORD PLAY

Which word beginning with GRAN means:
1. A place for keeping grain? (7 letters)
2. Great power or rank; splendour of living? (8 letters)
3. A kind of rock? (7 letters)
4. A large country house with farm buildings attached? (6 letters)

GRAN

GRANDAD   GRANOLITHIC   GRANULATED   GRANTOR   GRANNOM   GRANGER   GRANT   GRANIFEROUS

ODD GRAN OUT

In these four pictures of Granny, one is very slightly different from the others. Which one is it?

ANSWERS

P. 13 Find Granny and Grandpa

A	P	D	N	A	G	R	A	N	N	P	A
P	N	A	R	G	R	A	N	N	D	P	P
D	A	D	G	R	A	N	D	A	P	A	D
N	G	G	R	R	N	G	R	R	A	Y	N
A	R	R	A	A	A	A	N	A	N	N	G
Y	A	A	N	N	N	N	Y	N	D	R	R
D	N	N	D	G	M	N	N	N	A	G	A
R	D	N	A	G	A	N	N	Y	R	N	N
A	A	A	P	D	R	Y	G	R	N	A	D
N	G	A	P	D	N	A	R	G	D	N	N
N	R	D	P	A	G	R	A	R	A	N	Y
Y	N	N	A	D	A	D	N	D	G	N	N

P. 14/5 Cycle Ride
There are 6 differences between the two pictures.

P. 20/1 How Many Grannies?
There are 3 grannies in the picture.

P. 26/7 Patchwork Puzzle
*1. Christmas tree. 2. Scissors. 3. Rugby ball. 4. Glove. 5. Flag.
6. Sock. 7. Cup. 8. Spanner. 9. Specs.*

P. 33 What?
*1. Fish and potatoes. 2. Cricket. 3. Elizabeth (the Queen Mother).
4. Get wet. 5. Anything you like! 6. A little otter (hotter). 7. One
with poor eyesight. 8. Eat it. 9. Tired! 10. Puts out his foot and
trips it up.*

P. 34 Family Party
*Ten. The grandmother is also a mother and a daughter, the
grandfather is also a father and a son. One of the daughters is also
a mother, and one of the sons also a father. The daughter-in-law is
also a mother, the son-in-law also a father.*

P. 38/9 Bird Table
*1. Sparrow. 2. Starling 3. Robin. 4. Blue tit. 5. Blackbird.
6. Thrush.*

P. 45 Crazy, Mixed-up Grannies!
Earnings.

P. 46/7 Picture Story
The correct order of the pictures is 4, 7, 3, 5, 9, 2, 8, 6, 1.

P. 59 Who's This?
Granny Smith!

P. 64 Wool Gathering
Ball of wool number 2.

P. 70 Sofa, so Good
Piece number 7.

P. 71 What Time Is It?
Twenty minutes to five.

P. 76 Granny Knots
Knot B will pull into a knot.

P. 78/9 Old Puffers
Squares B2, F5 and G3 are identical.

P. 82/3 Spot the Specs
There are 7 pairs of specs hidden in the picture.

P. 88 Word Play
1. Granary. 2. Grandeur. 3. Granite. 4. Grange.

P. 89 Odd Gran Out
Granny D is the odd one out because her coat is shorter.

WHAT'S THE DIFFERENCE BETWEEN FALSE TEETH AND A DEAD MOUSE?

IF YOU DON'T KNOW — UGH!!